Edited by Aaron Peters, Deborah Peters and Kathy Dupree

Cover art by Samantha Kelly

BORN AT HOME WITH BLESSINGS

A collection of birth stories

By Kathy Williams

I dedicate this book to my husband, who has been patient with me not only writing but every day of my life as a midwife. He has loved and supported me in my life's calling with his whole heart. I would not be where I am today without him, he is the love of my life.

Acknowledgements

Thank you to hundreds of families that have been a part in my collection of birth stories over the years. If your story in in this book or any future books, I hope you are pleased with my telling of it. I have taken care to never reveal any names. The names of chapters were chosen for the meaning, which I feel names the character of that story. Thank you to Lily Harvey, for getting me started in my journey. Thank you to Jennifer Meadows, Gaylea McDougal, Celesta Bargatze, Heather Munoz, Talitha Mills, Heather Wilson and all the Nova Birth doulas that invited me to their births as an assistant. Thank you, Samuel Simpkins for your thousands of photos to document my births.

Thank you to my family, for allowing me to do what I needed to and encouraging me. You always made my "job" a normal part of us all. Thank you to all who have listened to me tell my birth stories over the years and encouraged me hundreds of times by saying, "You should write a book!' Thank you to Aaron and Deborah Peters who offered to edit text and design the cover for me. Thanks to Kathy Dupree for editing and Samantha Kelly for the watercolor picture for the cover. Again, thank you David Williams for being my Hubby and best friend. You have always encouraged me to write my stories down. I appreciate the many hours of proof reading and crying with me as we read the stories we had lived.

Table of Contents

17. Mira – One who is prosperous and peaceful
18. Gemma – A girl who is treasured like a precious stone
19. Tristan – sorrowful, sadness
20. Louanna – Gracious warrior, brave woman

SHAUNA

God is gracious

It was a cold January day and the beginning of
a new year. I had only missed one birth because of
snow and ice over the years, but it was always
discussed with the families due in the winter. That
year, I still had one December baby left that was
not delivered yet. It really needed to happen since
she was two weeks past her due date and usually
had larger than average babies. It ran in their
family. Her mother and some of her sisters grew
big healthy babies too; they were monitored for
gestational diabetes and were always normal. The

"overdue" thing seemed to run in the family as well. It was just normal for them.

I had done several home visits that day, my first day of work that year. I drove between appointments in a cold car; the farms in this community were closer together than some. All the houses were so toasty warm from their wood burning stoves. I wore a heavy sweater and scarf and took them off at each house when I arrived, then put them back on to drive to the next one; layers went on and came off all day. That was usual for me in the winter. I also kept an emergency blanket and pillow in my car and snacks in case I got stuck in snow or ice.

I arrived at her house for a regular prenatal and the overdue talk at about one-thirty in the afternoon. They knew what to expect and her husband was there too. We talked about castor oil, she really didn't want to take it, but we knew the baby needed to come out and we thought it was probably eleven pounds by now. She was more than ready to hold her little one, or big one!

Her husband brought her the castor oil, opened the bottle and handed it to her with a chaser. She smiled at him and drank it without hesitation. I still had another appointment to do, so I left and planned to come back after I was finished. When I returned, she was seeing results from the oil and a buggy ride, so I decided to sit in my car and do some office work while they went about their normal chores and tended the children. "It's either gonna go, or not." her husband said.

By the evening, I needed to use the outhouse which was in the back, (and very cold), so I stopped in the house to see how things were going and listened to the baby. She was still not having very many contractions, and we all thought that labor may not happen. They sent the children to the grandparent's house to spend the night and scheduled a driver to take them in to be induced at the hospital, in the morning. I left to go find somewhere to eat and when I got back again, labor was still very slow but had gotten more consistent, so her husband was not comfortable with me leaving to go home. I went back to my car to try and get some sleep. It was quiet in the country, so when I started my car to warm it up occasionally, it seemed so loud. I was thankful for my blanket and pillow! I had a hard time falling asleep, my mind was busy, but I finally did doze off.

I was startled from my sleep by a knock on my car window. It was her husband telling me to come in the house. I tried to clear my head and focus as I followed him in. He told me that she had been having hard contractions for about fifteen minutes. When I listened to the baby, it sounded great and mama certainly sounded serious. I put down the times and made a few notes on the chart while I listened to her labor. I could tell a lot by listening to her breathe and I could estimate the length and intensity of contractions. Nine minutes after I walked in the door, I could hear that her body was ready to push, so I put my work down and grabbed my gloves. Just a couple of minutes later her water broke and before I could listen to the baby's heartbeat, it was born! I was in the house for only twelve minutes, and they had a baby! It was certainly good that I didn't go home! Her eleven-pound baby was pink and crying, perfect in every way. A half hour later, she delivered a huge placenta, over two and a half pounds! The grandmother missed the birth, but her buggy arrived shortly after the baby and she was there to do all the usual things that grandmas do afterwards. We were all amazed at how fast it was and thankful that I was only a few steps away when this one finally decided to come out!

After the excitement was over, things were tidied up and mom, and mom was tucked into bed with her baby. I gathered my things, loaded my car, and left to go home. It was a cold night and frost had already covered my car windows. I had to wait for them to defrost so I could see. The drive was dark and quiet, and the roads were empty. Even though I had slept a while in my car I was still tired. Working all day and being on call for several hours, was emotionally exhausting.

The older I get, the more it affects my physical body too. When I finally pulled into my driveway (I hadn't been home in twenty-two hours) my Hubby was on his way out to go to work. We said our goodbyes and sweet dreams, and I crawled into bed just as the sun was coming up. With a thankful heart, I easily slipped into a sweet sleep.

I had only been asleep for a few hours when my phone rang. I jumped straight out of bed, like I always did, and as I said "hello" the daylight confused me for a second, then I realized that I had been up all night... The call was from a dad whose wife was just a few days before her due date. I got up, dressed and headed back to the same community I had been at earlier that morning, and the day before.

When I arrived, there was only her and her husband at home, she was lying on her side in the bed. She usually labored quietly, so it was hard for me to tell how serious she was. I sat down on the floor to do chart work and listened to her labor. She remained quiet, but I could hear her breathing change when she had a contraction. Dad was sitting on the bed with her and we talked about this and that for about a half hour. Then she delivered, as quietly as she had labored, a strong, healthy beautiful baby. It took several minutes before dad asked if it was a boy or girl, and several more before mama looked. Finally, she announced that it was a girl! Sweet and perfect, and we all smiled. Within the hour, dad had made us egg sandwiches, and we all sat in the bedroom and ate breakfast together while she nursed her baby. I remembered the other births I had attended for this family and felt very blessed to be in their home, welcoming another baby!

Once again, I packed my bags, cleaned up the birth laundry, passed out hugs, and headed to my car. While I drove home, in the sunshine this time, I pondered the two births. I had been at work or in my car for about thirty-four hours. I had driven one hundred and sixty miles and my brain was fuzzy from exhaustion. These babies were born eight hours apart on the same day. One was two weeks late, the other was three days early. One was overnight, the other was during normal business hours. I had served these two families, a total of ten times now. My heart was so full. When I got home, my Hubby was coming in from work too, and was surprised to hear that I had been to another birth. I made us some supper and tried to relax before going to bed early. After all, I did have several other moms that could call me that night! I wondered, if this was an indicator of how my year would go? Maybe, maybe not, but it was a great way to start that new year. I was blessed beyond measure by what God had given me to do.

"Wherever you go and whatever you do, will be blessed."
Deuteronomy 28:6 New Living Translation

AMMON

The hidden one

They were expecting their third baby with me.
Home visits had usually been at my house over
the five years that we had known each other,
mostly on her husband's day off. I had visited their
homes occasionally, in different places, since they
had moved for each pregnancy. This time, I was
the one that had moved. Their first two children
were born at my Hunters Lane house, and now
this one would be born at my new house. My
Hubby and I had bought twenty-three acres and
built a house; we had been in it for about a year
when I started seeing them with this baby.

The older children came with them and when they walked into my office and guest room, they always got comfortable, like most children do. Coats and shoes came off and they didn't hesitate to show me their latest toy or ask questions. Sometimes they told me all about what they did that week or about a movie they had watched. It was nice for me to know that they are comfortable with me and felt free to be themselves in my home. I always got hugs when they left.

This pregnancy was similar to her others and went well. She was healthy, and her body knew how to grow a baby. The only thing that was not textbook perfect, was that she tended to carry her babies a little longer than the national average. Her firstborn was more than two weeks past her due date with a sixty-hour labor, but she did deliver a perfectly healthy baby at home naturally! The second baby was a similar story except that her labor was only four hours. Hallelujah! We spent some time at our visits discussing how different the first two births had been and wondered how this one would be.

At two in the morning a phone call drew me out of a deep sleep, "Contractions are hard and regular, and we are headed to your house!" When I hung up, I tried to clear my head from sleeping and to think what day of the week it was. Did I have appointments that needed to be canceled? It was Friday, the thirteenth, the day before Valentine's Day. I called my assistant to come while I put on some appropriate clothes and threw my hair up in a bun. I brushed my teeth, then went to the other end of the house to get the guest room ready. I turned on the flood lights and unlocked the door to my office. Then I thought I should probably fill the bathtub in case she wanted to get in. The hectic forty-five minutes since their phone call had me wide awake now. I sat in the office and waited for them since I had everything ready.

When I saw the car lights, I stepped out on the porch to see if she needed help. She got out of the car slowly and had to stop a couple of times coming up the sidewalk. "You look serious," I told her. She shook her head yes saying that she was thankful it was a shorter drive to my house this time. She got in the door and slowly made it to the bathroom, while her husband grabbed the bags from the car. We listened to the baby and it sounded great. Her contractions were strong, lasting a long time and one on top of another. There was not much time to catch her breath between them, but she was doing great. I knew that this wouldn't take very long. Fifteen minutes later she started pushing, still on the toilet. She wanted to get in the tub but was having a hard time moving between the contractions, they were so close together. She stood up just before her baby's head eased out; it was still covered with the bag of waters. Such an unusual thing to see, the fluid swirled around the baby's face like a snow globe. I grabbed a towel to catch the baby, so he wouldn't fall into the toilet. The next minute, the baby was born with a tidal wave of amniotic fluid and crying loudly to let us know how strong he was! A few minutes later my assistant arrived, she stood at the bathroom door and looked disappointed that she had missed the birth. She told us that she drove as fast as she could, but we explained that this one just came too fast. The two-hour labor was over, and it was still dark outside!

It wasn't very long after that, I heard my Hubby get up and make coffee. He was getting ready for work and could hear the baby crying and birth goings on in the guest room. I came into the kitchen to say good morning and make eggs and toast for the new parents and the midwives too. This was a homebirth tradition for families that had their babies at my house. I made them toast from my homemade bread and scrambled eggs. There have been a few exceptions over the years, but this family has enjoyed toast and eggs at my house several times! We sat around and talked, my assistant did the newborn exam and weighed the baby. There were lots of pictures taken and phone calls made. My hubby went to work, my assistant went home, and then the mom, dad and new baby left to go home too. I changed the sheets on the bed, cleaned the bathroom and took out the trash. Then I had a shower and crawled into bed to get a couple of hours of sleep.

It was all in a day's work, or a night's work, and sometimes it encompassed both. I replayed the birth over in my head and would debrief by going over it later with my assistant. "Were there things that could have played out differently?" Yes, almost always. I wondered how mom and dad's perspective differed from mine. I asked mama, at her first visit after the baby was born, "Is there anything you would change about your experience, or that you wish was different? Her reply was, "I wouldn't change a thing, it was just how it was supposed to be!" After I heard that, it made everything I do worthwhile. Then I smiled and filed this birth away in my heart, to be recalled at another time.

"Jesus replied, "I assure you, no one can enter the Kingdom of God without being born of water and the Spirit. Humans can reproduce only human life, but the Holy Spirit gives birth to spiritual life.""
John 3:5-6 New Living Translation

JESSICA

God sees all

Her history was sexual abuse. I could understand as a birth professional and on a personal level too. I knew that a history like hers could cause depression, anxiety and problems coping with birth sensations. I also understood that birth trauma at the hospital can cause the same issues or reopen the wounds and make the abuse feel real again. Her previous hospital birth had made her feel exposed and violated and she didn't want that experience again. She had dealt with her past and had a wonderful relationship with her husband. The abuse was not the issue anymore, it was how she had been treated during her hospital birth and she wanted a different experience this time.

From the first time we met, we were like old friends. I would never have known that she was an abuse victim if she hadn't told me. She was sweet and open, we talked about all kinds of things. I got to know their little girl as we did our home visits and her husband was there sometimes too. I was delighted to get to know this family and see how gentle and kind they were to each other. As we got closer to the delivery, she shared with me some specific things that bothered her about her hospital birth. I completely understood. I had worked labor and delivery for a while in my early years. I made my mental notes and felt like I could remember her triggers and not push any emotional buttons. We were connected and talked freely. I understood her pain and her healing and was excited to be a part of her new birth experience. I knew it would be perfect this time!

Early in the spring, I got the phone call that she was in labor. As I drove there, through city traffic, I thought about all the things she had told me. I wanted to be careful to not say or do anything to make her feel uncomfortable. I arrived at her house around noon and I never offered to check her since that was one of the things that had made her feel tense before. I asked her if I could listen to the baby, she nodded yes. I made eye contact with her and we both smiled. "Baby sounds great!" I said. Then I sat on the floor to do my paper work and watched her while she did what she needed to.

She and her husband stayed face to face; she looked into his eyes for comfort and focused on him for her strength. She stayed completely clothed as she moved from standing and swaying, to the toilet and then to the floor on all fours. I knew she was getting close because her groans were more intense now. It was just her and her soul mate, her husband and partner in life. They created this child together and would birth it the same way. She kneeled on the bedroom floor just outside the bathroom and I heard a serious bearing down with her next contraction. Then I told her that if she needed to push, she should probably take off her panties. Her husband helped her with that over the next few minutes, but it never really got done. The baby crowned with her panties almost to her knees, then he was completely out with the same contraction! Screaming, perfect and pooping all at the same time! He had been born so quickly that squeezing through the birth canal made him poop, and it landed in her panties. She and her husband greeted their newborn, cried and smiled and were in awe of how peaceful it was.

She had no vaginal exams, no exposure, no touching, just her and her husband, working hard, then they had a baby! As I got things cleaned up and got them settled into bed, we all laughed. How often can someone say, "My son pooped in my panties, while I was still wearing them?" I had never seen that before, and not again since. It was a beautiful birth and I was blessed by being invited to witness it.

For that birth, hands off was the issue, complete trust that I would not touch her without asking. Eye to eye contact was also important and words were not necessary at times, just my physical presence and an understanding heart. Total healing was the result in the end. Birth trauma was very real but had been overcome and healed. Now she could help others to heal as well.

"God is our merciful Father and the source of all comfort. He comforts us in all our troubles so that we can comfort others."   *2 Corinthians 1:3-4*
New Living Translation

WENDY

Wanderer; family

It was the end of March when I had a whirlwind of births all on the same day. I had gone to the first mom's house the day before for a labor check and she had fizzled out, so I went back home. Then she called me to come back on her due date, late in the evening. I arrived at her house a little after eleven, with my assistant and a birth photographer.

That couple was having their second baby with me and I had enjoyed getting more familiar with them and their other children that time. I knew how this mom had labored before and what she liked and didn't like. She mostly did her own thing and focused on what her body was doing as she walked around in the living room and listened to affirmations. The atmosphere in the room was relaxed and dimly lit with only a few candles on the mantle. My assistant and I sat on the floor and did paperwork and watched the kids play. Just after midnight, I got a phone call from a dad whose wife's water had broken and they wanted me to come. Her due date was not for two more weeks and she wasn't having any contractions yet. I went to the kitchen to talk so that I wouldn't distract my laboring mom, and I told him that I was at a birth and couldn't leave, but I would call another midwife to go. When I returned to the living room, mama was standing and swaying and looked very serious. She had wanted pictures that time, so she was trying to stay in an open area for more room. After a while, labor seemed to slow down and she got a little bit discouraged. We thought maybe if she rested, things would pick up again.

At about four in the morning, things changed suddenly, and she wanted the tub, so she filled her bath and got in. The bathroom was only big enough for her husband to sit on the toilet beside her. My assistant and I and the photographer were all outside the door. Fifteen minutes after that, she pushed one time and delivered her baby girl. The little one was limp and pale, she didn't cry or respond to mama talking to her. I squeezed into the small area to feel the baby's heart rate, which was alright, but she was not coming around so I asked mama if I could give her a breath and she handed me the baby. Two breaths from my mouth and she let out a loud cry! I handed her back to her mom; she was strong and turned pink very quickly and we all thanked God for that.

I had gotten a phone call just before that baby was born from another one of my mamas that was two weeks past her due date. She was in labor and wanted me to come as soon as I could. I explained that I would leave my assistant with the mama that was delivering, after I was sure that everything was okay. She understood that I would be there as soon as possible. I was with the new mama and baby number one for about an hour, then I headed over to mama number two and left my assistant with number one. I was also in touch with the other midwife that I had sent to mama number three's house, whose water was broken, and labor was slow.

I arrived at the overdue mom's shortly after six in the morning and she was having strong contractions, standing in the bathroom. Four days before that, she had gotten an ultrasound and her baby had been laying sideways. I listened to heart tones and made sure he was head down and we were all relieved that he was. Mama moved to the bed and pushed for ten minutes, then delivered her strong healthy eight-and-a-half-pound baby boy! He was almost two pounds less than her previous baby had been. I had only been there for thirty minutes when he was born. Everything was perfect, so I took care of all the normal things that I did after a birth. My assistant who had been at mama number one's house joined me at mama number two's. Then, I got a call from the midwife at mama number three's house; she told me that labor was active, and I should probably come. So, I left around ten o'clock to go join her and my assistant went home exhausted after being up for more than twenty-four hours.

On my way to the third mama's house I got another phone call. It was mama number four and she was having contractions and in early labor. She was one week past her due date and was having her second home birth after a c-section with her first baby. I stopped by my house to change clothes, grabbed something to eat in the car and thought about the fourth mama in labor. I arrived at the third mama's house and the midwife that had been there filled me in on what had been going on. I could tell that labor was serious, and a few minutes after I arrived, she stood and delivered her eight-pound baby girl! She cried immediately and was strong and perfect even though she was two weeks early. Mama number three did great and had her mother and mother-in-law there along with her husband to help with things. I was tired and thankful for the help. It was only one in the afternoon and I had witnessed three births in the past eight hours, and still had another mom in labor. My midwife friend was a huge help for me that day; we both left there and went to mama number four's house.

When we got to the next house, mom was struggling with contractions; her husband was encouraging her, but she was tired. I completely understood as I felt the exhaustion taking its toll on me too. My midwife friend told me that she could watch mom and listen to the baby, if I would sleep for a bit. About an hour later mom was still struggling and wanted to be finished with labor so the other midwife offered to break her water and she and her husband agreed. They walked around the house and went outside over the next couple of hours while I cat-napped on the couch. Just after dark, when she got back on the bed and pushed, the baby's heartrate dropped so we put the oxygen on mom. It was concerning but we continued to listen, and it didn't drop anymore. Mama was strong and had her baby out within ten minutes. His umbilical cord was wrapped around his neck three times, but once I got him untangled, he cried like a champ! Mom, dad and the midwives all praised the Lord for a strong healthy baby boy!

My friend and I left the fourth birth just before midnight almost exactly twenty-four hours after I had arrived at the first labor. It had been a birth marathon Saturday! The other midwife and I talked on the phone while we drove, to keep each other awake. The night air was chilly, so I had my car window down a little, which helped me be alert, but it was dark and there weren't any vehicles on the road. I had never done four births in twenty-four hours before and was completely exhausted. I had driven more than three-hundred miles when I finally got home. My birth bags were empty, but once again my heart was full to overflowing. They were four very different births and each one was a story to be told.

"Yet those who wait for the Lord will gain new strength; they will mount up with wings like eagles. They will run and not get tired, they will walk and not become weary."   Isaiah 40:31 New American Standard Bible

EMILY

Industrious and hardworking

I had attended births for this family before. She didn't usually have long or difficult labors, but this time started out a little differently. We had counseled and fine-tuned her supplements and addressed the issues from previous deliveries or labors. We discussed the mental and emotional concerns of labor and addressed fears and expectations during her home visits.

It was in the springtime when she called me on a Thursday morning to say that she had been having contractions through the night. We decided that it would be good to hear the baby and see where she was in labor so that we could plan the day. I arrived for a labor check at eight in the morning, dad had not gone to work yet, and all the children were excited to be waiting on their new baby sister. I felt mom's belly for how the baby was laying so I could listen to the heartbeat and discovered that the baby was breech. I had no doubt that mama could deliver a breech baby without complication, since she had given birth naturally, several times before, and I had experience with that kind of birth. We talked about the differences of a breech birth from a head down baby in detail, the main thing was the pushing instructions. I also explained how the hospital treated breeches and that most were c-sections. She and her husband knew what to expect and they had prayed and decided to stay home to have the baby. She was dilated too much for me to leave, even though she was not having as many contractions as she did through the night. My assistant and I thought we should stay close by, so we went into town and walked around in several stores.

By three in the afternoon, she hadn't made any progress. She had gone about her normal day and had very few contractions, but her water had not broken, so we waited. After several more hours it was still the same story. She had managed the children, fed them, gave instructions to helpers and labor had stopped during the day. My assistant and I went to the store, had dinner at a restaurant and came back. Baby sounded good, but mom still had no change in dilation, so we all decided to try and get some sleep. The children were all in their beds, grandmother and aunt were close by and the midwives went to their cars.

During the night, while the house was quiet, she started with regular contractions again. They did not progressively get longer or closer together, so it was most likely Braxton Hix and not labor. We checked on her a few times, the baby sounded great and we thought that labor would keep going this time. Then on Friday morning when the children woke up and needed to have breakfast, mom started tending to the needs at hand. Soon after that we noticed that she wasn't having contractions anymore. She decided to take a walk around the neighborhood, maybe it would get things going again. It was a nice spring day, so we all walked with her. When we got back to the house, she continued with her daily duties and had no contractions. We all went to bed again to try and sleep, hoping and praying that labor would happen. Everyone was getting discouraged.

We had been in with her through the third night, again with regular contractions, while everyone in the house slept. As soon as the children got up and the morning routine started, contractions stopped. When I hadn't seen her have a contraction for more than an hour, I told her that I was beginning to see a pattern here. She said, "me too!"

I had to be the "mean midwife" and tell the grandmother and helpers to take the children all away from the house, go to the park, or walk around the block, whatever! This mom and her baby needed to connect and get serious. Three days of not enough sleep and intermittent contractions had been exhausting and everyone was on edge, ready to have this baby out. Mom couldn't focus on what she needed to do with the distractions of everyday life and house guests too. The siblings were all frustrated that they had to leave but the adults planned to go to the park, and they all left after lunch. Contractions started soon after the house was empty and then she could concentrate on the job she had to do, and her body started working. She only had a small amount left to dilate but the uncertainty of how it would all play out was in the back of her mind. She had not seen breech birth before. What if she couldn't do it this time? What if this baby had something wrong with it? What if she did something wrong? The same questions entered every woman's mind as she was giving birth. Mom dilated quickly and pushed for a few minutes, trying to get her mind wrapped around it. She changed positions and was a little bit unsure of herself. Then, she decided, "I can do this!" Once she had set her mind on it, she worked with her body and pushed, then her perfect baby emerged from her mother's body, bottom first, then legs and arms; she kicked and squirmed the whole time. Then out popped her little head! She didn't hesitate to let out a loud cry and let us all know she was here!

Fifty-six hours after my assistant and I arrived at her house, this hard-working mama had her baby. She had contractions mostly alone for three nights in a row and did her normal work and took care of her children during the day. Her baby was born late Saturday night, after all the other children were asleep. This labor was difficult to figure out at first, but mom needed her space, with her husband and midwife and no other distractions. She showed tremendous strength, endurance and patience, and learned that it was okay to not have an audience at her birth. My assistant and I both learned a few things too and everyone there was blessed!

"I have fought the good fight, I have finished the course, I have kept the faith; in the future there will be laid up for me the crown of righteousness,

which the Lord, the righteous judge, will award to me on that day; and not only to me, but also to all who have loved His appearing." 2 Timothy 4:7-8 *New American Standard Bible*

HOPE

One who has expectations through faith

It was on Mother's Day when I had phone calls from two different moms in labor. The first call came before daylight and was from her husband, not the mom herself; she had been having contractions since midnight and they were ready for me to come. I got up, dressed and headed out in the dark. As I drove, the sun was coming up on the horizon across the spring wheat fields, and I got the second call from another mom who had also been having contractions all night. She had planned to go to my house, so I called my assistant and my midwife daughter to meet her at my house and I went to the first mom.

There was not much traffic through town on that Sunday morning and the sunrise was beautiful over the skyline. When I arrived at the couple's house, I got my birth bags in from the car and we visited for a little while. Her contractions had gotten further apart, and we thought is was probably due to her being tired since she had not slept much during the night. So, she laid in the bed and tried to sleep but that didn't last very long; then she got up and went to the shower. When the hot water ran out she moved to the birth ball in the bedroom. The kids were going about their normal activities, and the grandparents came over for a while. Mom hadn't eaten yet, so she and her husband made eggs and biscuits for breakfast. She continued to walk around the house because she couldn't really sleep anymore. She moved from one comfort measure to the next, and they talked to the children about watching their new baby being born, which they had already been prepared for. Mom's water broke after lunchtime and then labor got more serious; she stood in the shower then got on her hands and knees in the tub. Pushing that time was hard for her, she couldn't quite find the right place, so she decided not to have the children in the room. For over an hour she went from the birth ball to the shower and on the bed, then her body took over and she worked with it. Standing in the shower she pushed out her baby's head, then we had to wait a couple of minutes before his shoulders came out. He was a big boy! He cried right away, and mom and dad were so glad to see him!

Meanwhile, back at my house, the second mom and dad arrived, greeted by another midwife and assistant. Her contractions had stopped while they were driving. The couple really didn't want to go home without a baby, since she was past her due date already. They went into town to walk around and take some castor oil, while they worked on getting the contractions going again. They stayed in touch with my daughter but didn't come back to the house until three in the afternoon. (By the time I heard that, I already had the first baby, so I thought that I would have time to get things cleaned up and drive home before she delivered.) She was having contractions when they got back, so she wanted to get in the tub. A short time after she got in, her water broke. The baby had a bowel movement inside, so the tub water looked muddy. The other midwife had mom get out of the tub, in case the baby needed help breathing when it was born. Mom pushed on the bed for fifteen minutes and delivered a healthy baby boy one hour and forty-five minutes after they got back, that was a quick labor! The two babies were born only one hour apart.

While that was going on at my house, I was still at the first mom's house. I took care of the placenta and got mama cleaned up and tucked into bed nursing her new baby, surrounded by her husband and their other children. The I left to go home. I talked to the midwives at my house on the phone while they took care of the second mom and had her cleaned up and in bed when I got there. It was perfect timing to enjoy scrambled eggs and toast with my house guests and talk about our day. The four mamas in the room combined, had given birth seventeen times. It was a beautiful way to spend Mother's Day, helping two women become mothers again. At the end of the day we were all blessed.

"By the God of your father who will help you, and by the Almighty who will bless you with blessings of heaven above and blessings of the deep that lies beneath, blessings of the breasts and of the womb." Genesis 29:25 New King James Version

BOAZ

Swift and strong

I have served a few families that lived in the same county as my oldest daughter. It was always nice for me to do home visits with my clients and then get to visit my grandchildren too. It was convenient to have my family close by when those moms were in labor, sometimes I stayed at my daughter's house, if I needed to sleep or just wait. I had attended three births for one mom and dad in that county. The dad usually caught the baby, but it was nice to have an extra set of hands available, just in case. They already had several children when I met them for the first time. Over the years, I visited their home many times and their older children got to know me as well as the younger ones. The last birth that I attended for them was on my Hubby's birthday!

That family's oldest daughter called me when she was expecting her first baby. I was excited to be asked to attend her birth; I had watched her grow up and had known her for ten years. What a blessing for me to be back in touch with the family, and to be at the birth of their first grand baby. The young couple lived with her parents the first couple of years after they were married, and I knew that house well. She borrowed my birth pool for labor and delivered her firstborn quickly. It took longer to set up and drain the pool than it did for her to have the baby! She picked her baby up out of the water herself, and I didn't even get my hands wet before she had her baby in her arms. It was beautiful!

The young couple had bought a house before they had their second child. It was still close to her parents and my daughter too, so I combined my home visits with grandchildren visits and just spent the day in that county. I started her home visits early in the year while it was still cold and one visit I remember there was ice and snow on the roads. We had a very wet spring that year and it seemed that every time I went to her house it was raining or muddy. My daughter always had a big cookout for my son-in-law's birthday over Memorial Day weekend, which happened to be the month before this mom was due. That weekend, I went to do her home visit on a Saturday and got to see her parents, brothers and sisters too. Everyone was excited to be waiting for a new baby.

Early labor started with her water breaking before dawn. She waited to call me until after daylight to let me know, since she wasn't having any contractions yet. I looked over her chart again and this baby was going to be eighteen days early. While I was having my coffee and checking to see if I needed to change appointments for the day, I realized it was my anniversary! My Hubby and I had gotten married on my dad's birthday thirty-eight years ago. This was a special day to be attending a birth for a special family.

Around lunch time I checked in with her, and she still was not having contractions. We talked about the time limit of waiting for labor since her water was broken and that could cause a greater risk of the baby getting an infection. We had twenty-four hours to be in active labor, so I gave her a list of things to try that could get contractions started. The time limit would be up during the middle of the night, so she and her husband talked and prayed and decided to go ahead and take some castor oil. They didn't want to take any chances on the baby getting sick or having to go to the hospital. Within a couple of hours, she was having contractions and setting up the birth pool. I was already at my daughter's house close by.

At supper time her mother called me to say that they were ready for me to come over. It only took me about twenty minutes to get there, and I walked in to her pushing in the pool. I quickly dropped all my bags and looked at my watch. Her mother was standing in front of her by the pool and encouraging her. I listened to the baby and he sounded great. I turned around to lay my doppler down and mom said, "the baby's head is out." I had only been in the house two minutes! I had a pair of gloves in my hands, but before I could get them on she was picking her baby up out of the water and we all praised the Lord for a perfect, healthy and crying baby boy! We got her out of the pool, dried off, dressed and into bed while dad drained the pool and got everything cleaned up. A half hour later, she was eating and nursing her baby, with a satisfied smile on her face!

I stayed for a couple of hours and visited with old friends and talked about old times. I told them that it was my anniversary, as I got my bags ready to take to the car. Everyone wished me a happy anniversary then I went to take a load to the car. My birth pool was clean and bagged up for me to take too! I told them that I would call to check on them the next day, but if they had anything come up before that, to call me. So, I hugged everyone and left to go home. While I drove through the city, watching the sunset, I thought about the family and all the births I had attended for them, five so far. I smiled, thinking about the sweet blessing that they were to me.

It was about nine o'clock that night when I got home. There was no romantic dinner or date night, but after thirty-eight years of being man and wife, it was okay. Hubby asked me how the birth went, I asked him how his day was, and we talked for a few minutes about our wedding day and all our other anniversaries. We did that every year. Then we went to sleep; after all, it was only the middle of the week and the next work day was another one to be blessed.

"So, God was good to the midwives, and the people multiplied and became very mighty. Because the midwives feared God, He established households for them." Exodus 1:20-21
New American Standard Bible

Keoni

God's gracious gift

The couple was having their first baby and had gotten my name from some friends that had home births with me. They were excited about the pregnancy and were already making plans for the new addition to the family. They lived near me, so it was not hard to do her home visits when dad was there too. Their baby was due on my mother's birthday.

I visited them ten times through her pregnancy and each time, answered questions and helped them learn about having a baby at home. They were also doing their homework and talking to friends that had births at home and about how they went. Her husband did some training classes out of town, then during the summer he joined the military. When he left for boot camp they knew that most likely he would not be home when the baby was born. She made plans for her mother to be her coach during labor, and to have her husband on the phone when she was delivering.

It was Father's Day. I had been to church and then enjoyed lunch with my Hubby, our children, and grandchildren, celebrating the day for dads. It was seven in the evening when her mother called me; she said that her water had just broken. When I asked about contractions, she told me that her daughter had taken castor oil at noon. I got my things together and called my assistant to meet me over there. I thought about the last few home visits I had done with her, and she had never mentioned that she wanted to try to start labor. I always told my girls if they wanted to take castor oil, to call me first and be sure I wasn't already at a birth or had someone else in labor. I guessed that the subject had not come up during our appointments.

My assistant and I got to her house and found her in the bathtub and vomiting. Her mother was giving her water and told us that she hadn't eaten dinner. We offered her a few things, but she couldn't eat. I checked her and listened to the baby; labor was active and she was managing well. The vomiting could have been caused by the castor oil or from labor progressing quickly. Only an hour later she was ready to push, so we got her out of the tub since the water was cold and not deep enough to deliver in. They got her husband on the phone and put it on speaker. She tried several positions before she found one that worked for her, kneeling beside the bed on the floor was it. She pushed a little over an hour, when we could see the baby's head, and we all started saying out loud what we could see. Dad was listening on the phone and we wanted him to experience the birth too. Five minutes passed as the little one eased her way into the world! She needed a little bit of help to start crying but it only took her a couple of minutes to be heard by her dad. "Happy Father's Day!" she said to her husband. We could hear him crying on the phone, but he stayed there for a few more minutes as mom described what their baby looked like.

I have worked with a lot of military families over the years. Sometimes we had to get creative so that dads could be present at the birth. Other times, dads caught their own babies with me on speaker phone. Moms always worked the hardest though at bringing their sweet babies in to the world, no matter who was there.

"The one who plants and the one who waters work together for the same purpose, and both will be rewarded for their own hard work."
1 Corinthians 3:8 New Living Translation

FLINT

Spark, lover of nature

The fourth of July, that was the week that my Hubby and I always planned a big family camping trip for our children and grandchildren at a State Park. That year we had rented campers for everyone, so we all had air conditioning! The park had a swimming pool and hiking trails, a nature center, and lots of July fourth activities for the kids. They had a parade through the campgrounds, which everyone looked forward to. We spent a full week this time, Wednesday to Wednesday. My Hubby, our son and the sons-in-law all had to go to work during the weekdays, but they did have the three-day weekend off. I had a baby due, so I would probably have to work at some point too.

I got the phone call at nine-thirty in the morning. "My water just broke, but I'm not having contractions yet." The family that was having their baby that day had first hired me for their fifth child. "It's probably going to be our last baby" they had told me, and they wanted to have a home birth that time. Now, five years later, they were having their seventh! I enjoyed spending time with them and their children too. My daughter (the midwife) was at their sixth baby's birth with me and had brought her six-month-old son with her. The children had asked the next morning, "where's our other baby?". They were disappointed because they thought they had gotten two new siblings, a boy and a girl!

My grandchildren, ranging in age, from twenty months to eighteen years, were excited about the festivities planned for that day. I spent the morning watching my grands play together and relaxing around the campsite. The dads were there too. They threw frisbees with some of the kids while others rode bikes, then we all went to the pool before lunch to cool off. I always kept the phone close by, waiting for my birth call. After lunch, the little ones had naps and the teen-agers walked around the whole campground. Later in the afternoon, all the grandchildren went to decorate their bikes and line up for the parade. The older ones helped the younger ones, and there was a long line of all ages of campers escorted through the campground, with balloons and noise makers. At supper time the birth call came, and I got ready to go to work. I was so excited to go welcome a new little blessing.

When I got to her house, she was just beginning to have strong and regular contractions. As they progressively got stronger, she threw up a few times. I saw women do this sometimes as a response to the hormone shift and the increasing intensity of labor over a short time. Nursing her two-year-old had made the contractions start very suddenly and since her water was broken, they were more uncomfortable. She sipped on an electrolyte drink to stay hydrated and used the bathroom frequently. She managed her labor very well, changed positions often and walked around the house. The other children were always well behaved while mama was birthing and watched a movie to keep them occupied. I had been there for only three hours when she pushed one time on her hands and knees and had a perfect, healthy baby boy! We could hear firecrackers going off outside in their neighborhood, like a celebration of the birth. It took a while to get all the excited big brothers and sisters to go to bed that night. But finally, the new baby was loved on by everyone and the fireworks outside stopped and they settled down.

Just before midnight, I packed up my things and left to go back to the campground. There were still some fireworks going on here and there, bright colors lighting up the night sky as I drove. I thought about how perfect this day had been. It couldn't possibly have been any better. I celebrated the fourth with my kids and grandkids and even got to watch the parade. The timing of the birth was perfect, and I got to celebrate with that family too. I saw fireworks while I drove and now I would get a normal night's sleep. It was mostly quiet when I got back to the park, but a few folks were still sitting around campfires. I climbed into the camper and tried to not wake anyone up; the air conditioner was humming like a constant white noise, so no one heard me come in. I got on my night gown, then crawled into bed and slept.

"A man's mind plans his way [as he journeys through life], but the Lord directs his steps and establishes them.   Proverbs 16:9 The Amplified Bible

CARYS

One who loves and is loved

She contacted me for the first time already half way through her eighth pregnancy. When I met with her and her husband at my house, their story was like many I had heard before. They had the first couple of babies at the hospital, then went the home birth route for the later ones. The midwives that they had in the past tended to get nervous over the size of her babies. She had only delivered one under nine and a half pounds, and that was her first! The rest of her newborns ranged up to eleven and a half pounds. The last few babies had either gotten stuck at the shoulders or were long labors. The couple believed in their hearts that a woman's body was created to conceive and grow a baby and that birth was designed by God to work perfectly. They trusted the process completely and had no reservations. It was important for them to have a midwife that believed and trusted the same things. We were all comfortable sharing our hearts, so they hired me.

Prenatal visits began in the springtime and were mostly at my house. The couple came together, without any of the children, making it their date day! We had lots of discussion about raising children, discipline, homeschool, eating healthy, making bread... occasionally other things would come up, like the summer garden, keeping bees and religion. Her pregnancy progressed normally, and her blood counts were always good. She was an average sized woman; her husband, on the other hand, was larger than average, well over six feet tall. (Which was probably the reason for her large babies!). After twenty years of marriage and seven children, they had a wonderful family and happy marriage.

During the last month of her pregnancy, I drove to their home for a prenatal visit. I wanted to be familiar with how to get there and go over birth supplies and plans. Late in the summer, the day before her due date, she called just before lunch to give me a heads up; she said that she was having some signs that it may be that night or the next day. A few hours later her husband called, "She is having some contractions but not too serious yet." We decided that since I had a two-hour drive, I should go ahead and make my way to their house. "No hurry," he said. I left my Hubby to get dinner for himself and dashed out the door. As I drove through Nashville traffic during rush hour, her husband called me again. "Her contractions are about two minutes apart, just wanted to let you know, but you don't need to rush." I thought, "What? No rush?" The rest of the drive I couldn't stop feeling like my phone would ring and I would hear a baby crying on the other end. I drove as fast as I safely could.

I parked my car, got all the birth bags out of the trunk and tried to enter the house quietly. All the children were in the den, waiting to hear a baby. I was thankful that I didn't hear one yet! I went into the bedroom where she labored quietly and talked to me during her contraction. Dad was calm and gave her sips of water. He had the towels and things all laid out and ready for the birth. I listened to the baby, who sounded perfect. Within five minutes, she told me that she was feeling pressure like she could push and they both insisted that I check her to be sure she was completely dilated. After I confirmed that she was, mom stood at the end of the bed and only pushed through one contraction. Dad was very attentive, so I didn't interrupt what the two of them had going. The baby was born easily, in the veil, since her water had not broken in labor. I gently pulled the membrane away from the baby's face and the clear fluid poured out on the floor, but no crying was heard. The heart rate and color were good, but the baby looked like she was asleep. Some parents get nervous over a baby that doesn't cry right away, but the umbilical cord was still attached, pulsing and connected to mom, so the baby was still getting the same blood and oxygen that she had been getting for nine months. I dried the baby and laid her on the bed in front of her mama. I told mom and dad to talk to their little one while I continued to stimulate her. Mom said, "We are so glad to see you! We love you so much!" The baby opened her eyes and cried immediately as her dad spoke to her too. It only took a minute and she was alert and crying!

I could hear all the other children outside the bedroom door. They whispered and listened with excitement! They had a new member of the family! Beginning with the older ones, they asked if they could see the baby. They were told that dad would come get them when they could come in. We got the mess cleaned up, got mom's gown changed and she settled into a clean bed to nurse her new baby. Then dad went to get the other children. They all came into the room with smiles on their faces and asked, "Is it a boy or a girl?"

Each face showed the joy in their hearts as they all gathered around their parents' bed. They laughed and talked about who she looked like and what her name would be... every member of this family loved this ten-and-a-half-pound baby girl!

After a while, the eighteen-month old, who had been the baby until now, woke from his nap on the couch and came to the bedroom door. Mama looked at him and smiled, but when he saw the new baby in her arms he broke down and cried. As he stood at the door and sobbed at the thought of having been replaced by a new baby, his oldest sister went over and picked him up. As she held him, she explained that he was a big brother now. The other children passed him around, each one held and consoled him. Every sibling made him feel loved as they, in turn, explained differently about how they all loved his new baby sister. After he was passed around the bed, mama handed the new baby to dad, and she held him too. As much as the new baby was loved, so was he! Not only by mom and dad, but by sisters and brothers too.

That was one big happy family, where every child knew they were loved, unconditionally, from the first to the last!

I made sure that all my paper work was done and confirmed a plan to come back. Then I loaded my car in the dark and started the two-hour drive home. It was late at night and I listened to worship music and played the whole beautiful birth story over in my head. The traffic was still busy through Nashville since it was an August Saturday night, but I didn't mind. I was still "high on birth", that full-heart feeling that I had after a baby was born and everything went well. I pulled into my driveway around midnight, the tree frogs were singing loudly as I went into the house. I hadn't eaten supper, so I had a snack and showered, then I slipped into bed next to my sleeping Hubby.

"Children are a gift from the Lord; they are a reward from Him. Children born to a young man are like arrows in a warrior's hands. How joyful is the man whose quiver is full of them!"
Psalms 127:3-5 New Living Translation

NAOMI

One who is pleasant, a beauty above all others

As a midwife, I have served several different Amish communities and have attended births for mothers and their daughters, sisters and cousins. These women worked hard during labor, as it took them to the very limit of what they could bear. Their husbands felt helpless, seeing their wives in pain and knowing there was nothing they could do make it any easier. Mamas were vulnerable and uncomfortable but never complained. It was an honor for me to be invited into their homes and have them in my home to witness their babies being born.

It was this couple's first baby. I always looked forward to meeting new families having their first babies. They usually called me again and again... since they tended to have many children. They believed that children were a blessing! Mama's pregnancy went normally, and I spent some time at each home visit to teach them about labor and what they could expect. They both came from large families with lots of brothers and sisters, so they trusted the birth process. We were all very confident that she would have a natural birth and a healthy baby.

Her husband phoned at two in the morning to let me know that her water was leaking, and she was having some contractions. They needed to call a driver to bring them down since they had planned to come to my house. It was the hottest month of the year, and they didn't have air conditioning or electricity. When they arrived a couple of hours later, the baby sounded good and she was managing her labor well. She wanted to get in the tub, but we thought it may slow things down, so she got into bed and tried to sleep between contractions. By two in the afternoon labor was harder, and she was in the tub. I hadn't checked her cervix yet because her fluid was leaking and until now, her contractions weren't very close together. After midnight she felt some pressure like she wanted to push so I checked her; she was almost completely dilated! But, the baby's head was not in the center, it was a little off to the side. She walked up and down the stairs several times and tried some other positions to help the baby's head to center.

During the next twenty hours she focused on her job at hand. A gentle and quiet spirit filled the birth room. She crawled on the floor and removed her apron and hung it on a hook. She removed her head covering and put it on the dresser, then she sat at the foot of the bed and leaned on her husband. She looked at him with love in her eyes as she rocked and swayed with her arms around his neck. She took off her dress the next time she changed positions and hung it up. No one spoke a word for hours. Slowly, one piece at a time, her clothes came off. In the afternoon, her hairpins were on the dresser, her slip was taken off, and she was mostly naked. She was so connected to her husband and to the comfort that she got from stroking his beard and smiling at him. He smiled at her too, but neither of them said anything. They were lost in each other and paid no attention to me or my assistant in the room. I watched the process unfold so sweetly while she pushed for several hours. She moaned and swayed, squatted and crawled. She moved with each wave and worked with her body, she drew strength from her husband as they smiled at each other. Only whispers were heard as the room got darker, but we never turned on any lights, then at sunset the couple delivered their firstborn. She too, was strong and beautiful, like her mother. The three of them cried, and my assistant and I did too! A beautiful new family was born.

The birth had covered four calendar days, and the baby was born on my son's birthday! It was one of my top ten longest births, but I saw labor in a whole new light. She never allowed anything to remove her from the job she had to do. Her husband was entirely focused on being and doing what she needed, and she gave him her complete approval as he supported her. I watched in awe of the relationship they had with each other, and now with their first baby. It was just the beginning for this lovely family.

"But the fruit of the Spirit is love, joy, peace, patience, kindness, goodness, faithfulness, gentleness, self-control; against such things is no law."   *Galatians 5:22-23 New American Standard Bible*

ZOE

Life giving woman

I met this young couple in July when they were expecting their first baby. I drove to their house on the mountain twelve times, for home visits and birth classes, over the next few months. My daughter (a photographer) even came with me once to do their prenatal pictures! She delivered in January, the mountain road was steep and snow covered. Labor started at night, and as I drove up the mountain, my car lights shined across the frozen ponds. The baby was born about sunrise, a strong healthy eight pounds! Then mama hemorrhaged, so we called an ambulance. I did all I could to keep her stabilized until the ambulance could get up the mountain. We could hear them go back down and come around to the other side. Almost three hours later, they were finally taking her to the hospital. I had gotten the bleeding under control, but her blood pressure was still low. She did fine and they gave her some blood and sent her home.

The second time she called me, I was excited to see her again. I have always claimed my repeat mamas as "my girls". The more babies they have had with me, the closer our bond got. My daughter (a midwife) did some of her home visits with me, since she lived close by and had planned to assist at the birth. The timing on this baby was the opposite time of year, and a daytime labor! I didn't get those very often. We had done all the usual prenatal things to prevent a hemorrhage this time and the baby was born beautifully with no extra bleeding. She delivered in the spring, and I did have an assistant with me, but it was my "photographer" daughter not the "midwife" one. She had done their pictures with their first baby and they knew her already. It was good to have extra hands that time.

With her last baby, I started seeing her in the spring when the mountain trees were in bloom. This time she would be due in the autumn. Once again, we planned for her to take supplements for anemia and bleeding to prevent a replay of her first delivery. Over the summer she had the usual other pregnancy issues, which we talked about and dealt with accordingly. She called me three different times during her second trimester with belly pain, shortness of breath and rectal bleeding. It was always a sudden onset and severe, so each time she went to the emergency room. The doctors assumed, since she was obviously pregnant, that it was gallbladder pain or labor, and they told her that the bleeding was coming from hemorrhoids. They looked at the baby on ultrasound and monitored for contractions. They even did a gallbladder ultrasound once and everything that they saw looked normal. Since no problems were found, except anemia, they sent her home all three times with iron pills. My home visits with her were always good; baby was active and growing and we worked hard on her anemia. The episodes she had puzzled us all.

Two days after her last emergency visit, she had another severe episode and went back to the emergency room again. She demanded that they figure out what the problem was, and it was obviously not pregnancy related. This time she saw a different doctor and ultrasound technician, and they must have taken her more seriously because they looked a little closer. Then, she called me to say that they found two masses on her liver, but they told her these were usually not malignant. However, they were sending her to A Nashville hospital by ambulance. A CT scan the next day revealed a mass on her colon too, so she was scheduled for a colonoscopy. They also gave her a blood transfusion for the anemia.

We stayed in touch daily. She got biopsies done and was diagnosed with colon cancer that had spread to her liver. The doctors recommended the baby be delivered within a week, so that she could start chemo. She went home from the hospital with a lot of things to process. She felt that since the cancer was so advanced, she needed to be aggressive and do the chemo. Her baby was doing great and growing. The little one would be six weeks early but should do fine and would be able to come home in a few of weeks.

This mama had been very active in her community with breast feeding support groups. She would not be able to nurse this baby after she started her chemo. So, she made a request to her friends and family that her baby would only get donor breast milk for the first year. Several other moms started pumping and freezing their milk to build a supply for this sweet baby.

The day of induction arrived. It was bittersweet in many ways. The hospital staff was prepared for a pre-term baby and the neonatal emergency team was on standby for the delivery. The room was peaceful, almost like being in labor at home, not tense at all. Mom was as calm as she had been with her other babies and looked forward to meeting this little one. Dad supported her like he always had. I was there, because after all, I was still her friend and midwife. We laughed and joked about all kinds of things through the morning, and the staff mostly left us alone. The nurse came in to check mama's cervix and said that labor was coming along nicely, then she told us that she was going to lunch. It wasn't long after she left that mom looked at me with "the look". "I think the baby is coming!" So, I lifted the sheet to take a peek, and yes, the baby was coming. Someone pushed the nurse call button and I put on gloves, just in case. It was just like at home, my midwife heart and hands kicked in and I was catching a baby. The team arrived as the baby was delivered. I started to step aside, but the doctor stood next to me and said, "Good job, you're fine. I need to get my gloves on." I laid a perfect, tiny, crying baby girl on mama's tummy as tears of joy filled all our eyes. Half the team that had been on standby rushed into the room, stayed for a few minutes to be sure that they weren't needed, then left. There was no emergency, just a normal birth! The doctor did her chores, then the nursery people took the baby, and the room was mostly quiet again. Mom and dad were lonely but knew that they could hold their precious daughter in just a few hours.

The four-pound baby girl did amazing and grew quickly on what little milk she got from her mother. I visited mama and baby in the hospital the following week and then kept in touch by phone almost daily. Once they got to take the baby home, I went to visit them on the mountain. In the six years that I had been going up there, I had seen it in every season and month of the year. My Hubby went with me this time; he had heard me talk about this couple and their beautiful mountain for several years and felt like he knew them too. The chemo treatments that she had gotten made her weak, and she couldn't do much of anything. The cancer was taking a toll, but she still had a sweetness about her and never complained. She never showed any fear, she was confident in her eternal life. A few days after I saw her, I got a phone call from her mother-in-law... "She passed away, this afternoon, laying in her husband's arms with a smile on her face." It was Tuesday, a beautiful, sunny autumn day. Just a few days after what would have been her due date. When I hung up the phone, my Hubby knew what had happened, then he held me as I cried. Sweet and beautiful, a mama, a baby, a couple, a family and my friend.

This baby girl was only fed breast milk until her first birthday. Every year, for I long time, dad stayed in touch with me around the same time of year. We even talked a few times and he sent me pictures of the children. He did a wonderful job raising them. I'm sure that he sees her mama in his daughter's sweet face, especially as she gets older. She would be so proud.

"For we know that if the earthly tent [our physical body] is torn down [through death], we have a building from God, a house not made with hands, eternal in the heavens."   *2 Corinthians 5:1 Amplified Bible*

DEANNE

Swift and beautiful

She texted me at just before three o'clock in the early morning, "I'm having some contractions, wondering if it's just false labor". I told her to drink some water and go back to bed. If she couldn't sleep, maybe it was early labor. This would be her third baby, but her first home birth. In the past, her labors had been off and on for about two days. She was also three weeks before her due date and she had not delivered a baby this early before. I laid back down to try and get a few more hours of sleep. My mind wandered... "Could this be early labor? Was she just being anxious?" I pondered the possibilities and second guessed myself. Still in my warm bed, my thoughts continued, "Did I say the right thing, or am I forgetting some small thing she said at a prenatal? Third babies break all the rules." Labor or not, one thing I've learned over the years is that once I got a call, there was no more sleeping for me.

One hour later she texted me again, "My husband filled up the birth pool, I am getting in, some of the contractions are painful." I asked if they were regular and how long they were lasting. Her reply was, "Yes, they are regular and lasting about ten seconds." I almost laughed out loud as I replied to her. "Real labor contractions usually last a full minute or more." Then I told her that if it was early in labor, getting in the pool could possibly make it stop. Ten minutes later, "The contractions are lasting thirty seconds now." Four minutes later, "I had two contractions that lasted forty seconds and were only three minutes apart." At this point, I was already getting my clothes on and told her I would come and listen to the baby and check her if she wanted. So, I grabbed all my bags, loaded my car and was headed her way. My estimated time of arrival was two hours after her first text. It was still dark, but there were a lot of farm vehicles on the road, more traffic than I had expected. My mind raced as I drove, "Should I have left earlier, or maybe I will get there and her not be in labor! She may not deliver for three more weeks!"

She texted me again, ten minutes before I was to arrive. "Let me know when you're here so I can let you in." That was a relief, I thought, no hurry. When I got to the stop sign in front of their house, my phone rang. Her husband said, "I can see something coming out. Could it be the bag of water?" I told him yes and that I was in their driveway. I quickly grabbed all my bags and headed to the door, all the while I thought, "I made it!" As I reached for the door knob, he opened it from the other side and said, "She's out!" Puzzled, I thought his wife was out of the pool, maybe. I asked, "the baby?" He shook his head yes as we walked into the bedroom. There mama was, holding her sweet baby girl and smiling! Baby was crying and we all just stood there for a minute, everyone was in disbelief that it was over so fast! I gathered my composure and started in with all my usual chores after a baby is born. As I filled out the paperwork, I realized, this was my firstborn's birthday! I was having a baby myself, on this day, many years ago.

Labor was complete in two hours, mama never had a contraction that lasted even forty-five seconds, and she was three weeks before her due date. This one just solidified my only rule about birth, "there are no rules!" but if there were, third babies would break them! I drove home watching the sunrise over smoking tobacco barns and empty fields, with a thankful heart.

"Give thanks to the Lord, for He is good! His faithful love endures forever."   Psalms 136:1
New Living Translation

IRENE

Peaceful woman

"The midwife missed my last 4 births." That should have been a clue, but then... I missed her first birth with me too! I have seen this a lot, not that I've missed that many, but it had happened. After mamas have had a few babies, they tended to ignore the early part of labor. Some women were better at it than others and some didn't pay attention until they were in transition.

This was her second baby with me. She usually had pre-labor signs earlier in the day or maybe the night before, then she delivered during the night while the children are asleep. It was nice for them to wake up to a new surprise in the morning! Even though she knew that her body was working, she continued with her normal chores and didn't pay much attention to it, until it meant business. We had decided at her last home visit that she would let me know during the early part, and I would come before it got serious this time.

She called me in the evening to let me know things were beginning to make her think it may be in the next day or two. I slept lightly that night, waiting for a call. In the morning, still feeling a bit tired, I started my day of home visits and office work. In the afternoon, I got a chicken on to cook for dinner and finished doing my laundry and got it all put away. Still no call. Just as my husband and I were finishing our dinner, she phoned, "It's not serious yet, but it's regular." I was going to take my time, load the car and go to her house. Her plan was to put her children to bed, then she thought that things would surely pick up.

I left Hubby to clean up supper dishes and spend the evening alone. The sunset across the corn fields was lovely and the autumn trees were pretty colors too. Most of the vehicles on the road were driving home as I was driving to work. Everyone was on their own journey. I got to her house at dark, pulled in the driveway and parked near the road; I didn't want the children to see my car and get excited. I could see the house in the distance from where I was, and the curtains were open. The family was all scurrying around and getting ready to go to bed, then the children went upstairs. After a few minutes, the lights went off in the bedrooms. It was so dark in the country and very quiet at night. I waited about another half hour before driving up to the house.

I got my birth bags out of the trunk, holding my flashlight under my arm. When I got to the door, she motioned for me to come in and said, "I think it means business now!" She soaked in a hot bath for an hour or so and things seemed to be progressing. When she got out we sat in the living room with her husband and talked. After a while we realized that the contractions were getting further apart. We decided that the bath worked well before, so she got back in the tub. That baby was certainly not coming as quickly as the last ones had. When she got out of the water, she walked around the house and I saw a change in her. She was quiet, but I could see that when she had a contraction her breathing changed and several times she said, "I'm ready to get this over with!"

I watched her pace, squat, walk and lean on furniture, but never a sound. Then, around midnight she got into bed and quietly pushed. I could see that her bladder was coming down in front of the baby's head, so I held it up and out came her perfect baby girl! Face up instead of face down. It's always fun to see the expressions that a baby makes as they are coming into the world. All the seriousness of the last hour turned into sweet words and smiles as she talked to her baby. I loved seeing the connection, the first few minutes after her baby was born, as I watched this mom and dad see their baby's face for the first time. I was in their bedroom, where people usually don't have visitors. The blessing for me was that they had invited me there to help them because they trusted me.

As I packed up my things to leave, her husband thanked me for coming. I also thanked him for having me there. Once again, I drove home in the dark hours, passing barns, cow pastures and such, but only one truck in the fifty miles. The stars in the black sky were millions. When I got out of the car I stood in the driveway for a minute, looking and listening; it was dark and quiet here at my farm too. I breathed in the fresh cool air and smelled the tobacco barns smoking. It wouldn't be daylight for a few more hours, so I should be able to get some sleep. My heart was satisfied as I slipped into bed next to my sleeping husband.

"The fear of the Lord leads to life, so that one may sleep satisfied, untouched by evil."   *Proverbs 9:23 New American Standard Bible*

PRIMA

The firstborn child

I had done this couple's home visit on her due date. I checked mama's vital signs and listened to the baby. They had planned to go to a Christian concert that evening after our appointment, so I didn't linger around very long. I had already done a few appointments that day and was ready for my work day to be finished. Traffic was busy on Monday afternoons, but I made my way out of the city and enjoyed seeing the colors of the fall leaves as I drove home.

I had just settled into bed that night when my phone rang; it wasn't quite eleven o'clock yet. Her husband told me that she had just started having contractions when the concert was over, while walking back to the car. They were coming regularly and lasting about thirty seconds. They were so excited! I gave them the usual instructions... go home, eat, drink plenty of water, go to bed and get some sleep. I told him that labor with first babies can take twelve hours or longer. I settled back into bed, and five minutes later my phone rang again. Yes, it was the excited first-time dad, telling me that the contractions were lasting a minute. Once again, I gave him the usual instructions and told him to call me back if her water broke or she couldn't talk to him through a contraction. They had studied childbirth books and were anxious to practice what they had learned.

I was barely asleep when the phone rang for the third time. I looked at the clock as I answered and got up to go to another room so that my talking wouldn't wake my Hubby again. It was exactly one hour from the last call and dad said, "She was sitting on the toilet and her water broke..." I asked the usual questions... "Was the fluid clear?" "Yes, it was." Is the baby active?" "Yes, it is." So, I told them to try to get some sleep, and that the contractions would probably get stronger now. I sat on the couch and debated with myself and decided to get dressed. I would not get any sleep, and my hubby wouldn't either; I would sleep better on their couch than here. We would all be more comfortable, just in case it went a little quicker than a usual first baby. I went to get dressed and yes, the phone rang again. I glanced at the clock, it had only been ten minutes. I said hello, the excited dad on the other end said, "She wants to push!" I explained that sitting on the toilet could make her feel pressure like she needed to have a bowel movement and told him that I was coming to their house. I could check things out when I got there and just sleep on their couch. He agreed, that was a great idea. So, I left Hubby asleep and headed out in the middle of the night.

I parked my car in the crowded parking lot and gathered my oxygen tank and birth bag and headed up the three flights of stairs to their apartment. I knocked, and he immediately opened the door. My first visual was her in the birth pool, in the dining room, and pushing with a contraction. In all the conversations we had had, over the last while, I had not been told that the birth pool was set up, or that she was getting in. Being a little confused, I quickly listened to the baby, who sounded perfect. Mom smiled at me and didn't look like she was in labor at all. She asked how long this could take, and I obviously had no clue since nothing about this whole two hours had been predictable. So, I suggested that we check her cervix and she agreed since they were eager to practice their relaxing, focusing, and all they had learned about how to manage labor. I put my gloved hand in the pool to check her just as she started another contraction. She stayed in position, so I checked as her body heaved for half a minute. When it was over, she asked me if she was in labor. I told her that she was in labor, completely dilated, and it would only take a few more pushes for the baby to be born!

They both looked as confused as I had been, then her husband asked, "When do we do the transition stuff? When is transition?" I explained to him that labor was finished, this was the end of transition, and the only thing left was to push out the baby. We were all three surprised, since none of this had been like the books said it would be! In just eight minutes they were holding their healthy baby, only two hours after they called me the first time. This one was a record, first baby labor!

She got out of the pool, dried and dressed, then settled into bed to nurse her baby. She kept telling me how easy this all was. She had prepared herself for it to be so much harder, even though they prayed for short and easy, like everyone did. I packed up my things, drained the pool, answered all their questions and went home. I was back in my bed before the sun came up. Hubby raised his head as I crawled into bed, "false labor?" I smiled and said, "Nope, they had a baby!" Not at all what I expected, but thankful beyond measure at God's faithfulness. His ways were always perfect!

"For His merciful kindness towards us, and the truth of the Lord endures forever. Praise the Lord!"
Psalms 117:2 New King James Version

ROSINA

Cherished; Like a rose

She and her husband were broken, emotionally. They were told by nurses and doctors, "You should never have another baby!" They had wanted as many babies as God would give them. Were the medical professionals right? Should they stop having children and be thankful for their three they already had? She grew big babies that had gotten stuck, and it scared the doctors. Were we crazy to think that we could have a baby at home? Was it too risky?

Our hearts connected immediately! They were like family from the first time we sat around my dining room table. The children were always like my own grandkids and they got to know my family as well as I got to know theirs. That year they did have a homebirth! A beautiful, challenging and redeeming birth. He was eleven pounds, and a blessing in every way. Two years later, they called me with the good news again!

Everyone was so excited to have a new little one on the way! She admitted to me that she was praying for a smaller baby this time. The ultrasound to confirm the due date revealed twins. Baby A was normal, baby B had some problems. Then the questions started again... Could we still do this at home? Was it too risky? We all had peace about staying home, but I had never experienced a birth like this and had no idea what to expect. They had never seen a baby with a birth defect like this either. Throughout the pregnancy, we did research on the possibilities and discussed what we had learned at each visit. They certainly didn't want a normal baby to be born in the hospital, and the more they learned and talked about it, the more they determined that they didn't want baby B to be born there either. Tests and monitors and people examining a baby with problems, sounded like a nightmare. So, they decided to go to a specialized obstetrician that could tell them what would happen in a hospital, given the diagnosis. They also had a consultation with a neonatologist that could explain the baby's specific birth defect.

That visit was the decision maker. They were told that baby B would not survive birth, that the diagnosis was not compatible with life. As hard as that was to hear, mom asked the doctor if it would make any difference where the child was born, hospital or home. He told them the place of birth would not make any difference. Then there were so many emotions! She was carrying a baby that would not live, and she was carrying a healthy baby that would. She and her husband decided on a home birth.

During her prenatal visits there were discussions about what possible other complications that could occur with twins.

Preterm delivery or extra bleeding were possible, but we passed all the hurdles with no issues. Throughout her pregnancy, the babies grew well, mom kept her blood count good, drank her water and walked. But mostly she cherished every movement she felt of the precious little one, knowing that this was the only time she would have with this child. We made a birth plan, just so we would be on the same page about resuscitation, comfort measures, etc. Still no one really knew how it would all play out.

Labor started four days before her due date, early on a Sunday morning. The timing was perfect! The only issue was that baby B was breech; this was not a huge problem since baby A would pave the way. We knew this mama could push out an eleven-pound baby and the twins were certainly smaller than that! During the entire seven hours of labor, both babies had strong and steady heart rates. The older children had been at their brother's birth, and they wanted to be in the room when the twins were born too, but mom decided to have them wait outside the door when she was pushing. There were only me and two other midwives with mom and dad. After a few pushes, baby A was born! Beautiful, crying and perfect in every way! The next hour was a bag of mixed feelings for us all. Celebration that the first baby was healthy, and out, but the dread of what was expected and the uncertainty of how it would be. We clamped baby A's cord and dad cut it, then she was wrapped and nursed while we waited. She settled down and was quiet and content, yet alert. It was like she knew that we were all waiting for her sister. Baby B had a strong heartbeat and mama was still having contractions, but the little one was slow moving down. After waiting an hour, she was finally born, feet first. Her heart rate and color were good, but she was a little limp and looked asleep. We had all agreed that we would try to resuscitate her if she was showing signs of life. The room was quiet as I gave her a couple of breaths and then she opened her eyes. She made a little frown and whimpered a weak cry! Everyone in the room cried too. "There you are!" I said. She had fair skin, plump red lips and was beautiful.

Dad cut the cord and we wrapped her up. The other children were in the room by then. We weighed and measured both babies; they were nine pounds each! We smiled at the answered prayer for a smaller baby that time. Then the room was just like any other home birth. The midwives finished up with mom while everyone else took turns holding Baby B and talking to her. She looked at the faces of her siblings and parents and made some pouty lips and grimaced a few times before she settled into sleep, like all newborns did. A couple of hours later, we could not detect a heartbeat anymore. It was such a loving and peaceful passing, from this world into the arms of Jesus. None of us knew the exact time. Did it really matter? What mattered was that she was never touched by anyone that didn't love her. She never left her mother's sight. She never felt anything painful, though the rest of us in the room felt plenty of heartache. Now we wait until we meet again, one day, when we can all smile.

"In peace I will lie down and sleep, for you alone, O Lord, will keep me safe."   *Psalms 4:8 New Living Translation*

MIRA

One who is prosperous and peaceful

This mama was having her first baby with
Blessings, though it would be her eighth child. Her
history was like many others, she delivered her
first babies in the hospital and the rest of them at
home. She always had them a few weeks early
and had quick labors, usually three to six hours. It
was the week of Thanksgiving, and I worked on
getting my meal planned since I always had a big
dinner for my family and friends at my house. I
spent Wednesday doing home visits and planned
to do some cooking in the evening when I got
home. I had seen that mama for a check-up and
had done her group B strep culture. Since she had
early babies it was important to know if she had

the bacteria. She was now considered full term and safe to have a home birth, so I was officially on call for her. I stayed up late that night and got everything ready for Thanksgiving dinner, I stuffed my turkey and put it in the oven before I went to bed.

At two-thirty in the morning, my phone rang. I jumped out of bed and the smell of a turkey cooking, got my attention as I answered. It was the husband of the mom that I just seen the day before, her water had broken and was clear, but she wasn't having any contractions yet. She planned to go back to bed and call me when they were ready to come to my house. I tried to go back to sleep but smelling the food cook made it hard. She called back at seven to say that they had a driver and were coming, but she was still not in labor. I had been up for a while, making vegetables and desserts. I thought the car ride would get her labor started, but when they arrived she still was not having contractions. Her strep culture was not processed since I had just done it the day before and she was uneasy about that, not knowing whether she had the bacteria or not. With her water broken for several hours the baby's risk of getting sick was higher, so the couple decided to do IV antibiotics. I got that done and let them settle in while I finished making dinner.

Around noon, she still wasn't having contractions, so she took some castor oil and vitamin C. My family had all arrived to eat, and my children helped get the food on the table. I checked on the mom every hour while we had our family gathering and ate. She was not having any labor signs, so we started another IV and gave her more antibiotics late in the afternoon. When that was finished she finally started having some mild contractions ten minutes apart. Within twenty minutes they had progressed and got closer together. A little later they had gotten hard enough that she wanted to get in the tub, so we ran the water. Just a few minutes after she got in, she was in active labor and eighteen minutes later had a crying baby girl. The baby's cord was wrapped around her neck tightly but hadn't caused a problem. Mom and dad were excited to have their sweet healthy little one and I was thankful that they were at my house.

I had a wonderful Thanksgiving meal with my children and grandchildren and had also put in a full day's work as a midwife. It was a blessing to have it all under the same roof. I fed the new parents turkey and dressing with all the fixings, instead of the eggs and toast that most get. My family put away all the food I had cooked and washed the dishes for me. We all had so much to be thankful for that day.

"In God we have boasted all day long, and we will give thanks to Your name forever. Selah." Psalms 44:8 New American Standard Bible

GEMMA

A girl who is treasured like a precious stone

I had been their midwife for all five of their
children and they had all been born during the
warm months of the year. They decided with the
last baby that they were probably finished, but
God had a better plan and He gave them one
more child to complete their family. What a
surprise to be having a December baby! They
always came to my house to have their babies
because she liked to use my bathtub. After four
beautiful waterbirths, they decided to have this
surprise baby at their own home. She had done
beautifully at laboring in the car each time, usually
during the night, but this time I would do the
driving. They lived almost three hours from me, so

I planned to stay at a hotel after the birth since I had no other moms due to deliver. Then I could do the one-day check before I went back home.

Her Husband called around four in the afternoon. "Things are beginning to happen, but it's not serious at all yet. We'll let you know when things pick up." They were going to send their children to the grandparents. I got things loaded in my car while I waited for another call. I packed my overnight bag and made sure my Hubby had dinner, then I started feeling a little bit of urgency after I had my chores done. I thought about the three-hour drive and the fact that this was baby number six. It was daylight though, and she usually started her labors around midnight, but I decided to start driving without hearing back from them. I was about forty-five minutes from their house when he called, "Contractions have been progressively getting more serious just for the past hour. The last few have been only a couple of minutes apart!" I drove a little faster then, and he was relieved to hear that I was close and not three hours away.

I arrived at their house and carried in all my bags. This time was different since I was used to waiting on them to get to my house. I walked in quietly and put down my birth bags and oxygen. The house was quiet too and there was a sweetness in the air. She was laying on her side on the couch, her husband was sitting on the floor in front of her, their foreheads were touching as they looked into each other's eyes. When a contraction started, she closed her eyes and breathed through it, and he breathed with her. I think he felt every contraction she had. They were connected and worked together to bring their baby into the world. I whispered a few questions and listened to the baby. Everything was good, so I quietly got things ready. Forty-five minutes later, mom walked slowly down the hall stopping every minute or so to breathe. Dad was walking backward in front of her and she held on to him every second. When she got to the bed, she laid on her side, in her husband's arms. It only took her three minutes to push out their perfect little surprise! They stayed there on the bed and fell in love with their new baby. Tears of joy filled their eyes and mine too; it couldn't have been more perfect!

I will always remember this couple; they were like my own children. I had watched them become parents for the first time and now their family was complete. For eleven years we built a friendship. They came to my house and brought their dogs and met my family. I visited their houses in two states and watched their family grow. I spent those years seeing the children grow and mom and dad mature as parents. They will always hold a very special place in my heart. Memories like these will be cherished long after I'm finished being a midwife.

"She opens her mouth in wisdom, and the teaching of kindness is on her tongue. She looks well to the ways of her household and does not eat the bread of idleness. Her children rise up and bless her; her husband also, and he praises her..." Proverbs 31:26-28 New American Standard Bible

TRISTEN

Sorrowful, sadness

I did her first prenatal visit in her twentieth week of the pregnancy. She and her husband had been in touch with me several times already, but I hadn't met them yet. She had been cramping and bleeding off and on, so I had sent her to the emergency room two different times. Ultrasounds had shown a healthy baby and all mom's blood work was normal. The doctors seemed to think that she needed progesterone and they had given her an injection at the hospital during her first visit to the emergency room. When I did their first home visit we went over her history and I checked blood pressure, urine, and listened to the baby. Everything looked good and she hadn't had any bleeding for a week. The baby was active and growing and mom was taking it easy and not doing many of her chores. There were plenty of family members to help with all that and her toddler too.

Monday the following week they phoned again to say she was bleeding and cramping like before. Once again, I told them to go to the doctor. The baby was active on ultrasound, but mom's cervix was dilated. The doctor sent them home without making it clear to them exactly what the problem was. Her husband told me that she started with all the normal herbal remedies to stop a miscarriage and stayed in bed. Just two days later, her husband called while I was doing my weekly appointments and asked if I would come and check on her, since the cramping had started up again. I told him that I would come over after I finished with all my other home visits.

I arrived at their house just before seven in the evening. The first thing I did was listen to the baby while we talked about her symptoms. I could feel her uterus contract like labor while I tried to find a heartbeat for several minutes. The silence was uncomfortable for us all; we could not hear anything. Her husband finally said, "We saw the baby moving all around on the ultrasound, just the other day!" I could not explain why I couldn't hear a heartbeat but we all knew the baby was not living anymore. I asked questions about what they had been told at the hospital. They didn't understand, so her husband went out to call the doctor. She had told them to call her if the problems continued. While he did that I checked mama to see if she was in labor and she obviously was. I suggested that we go to the hospital, since we couldn't do a home stillbirth with the pregnancy being this far along, and we also had no medical confirmation of the reason for the baby passing away. Her husband came in to get me and said the doctor would like to talk to me, so I put on my coat and walked out to the phone shed. I explained to her that I was a midwife and what had been going on. I told her that my client was in labor and I couldn't hear a heartbeat. She explained to me that the ultrasound she did, showed the placenta was already half separated. That was the connection between the mother and the baby; when it is separated before birth, the baby no longer had an oxygen supply and could not survive. The doctor was not surprised that the baby had passed away and the mom was in labor. She said she had told them that nothing could be done to stop the process at that point, before sending them home. I knew that the couple had not understood that part of it, so I told her that under those circumstances they would probably want to stay home to deliver the baby. She agreed that it would be fine and told me that this mama would only need to go to the hospital if there was too much bleeding. I went back to the house to explain it all to them.

We all decided that it would be comforting to look with my ultrasound, so they got together an overnight bag and I took them home with me. When we got to my house, I showed them around the guest room and got the ultrasound machine out. We saw no heart motion and the baby was still. We watched for a while, hoping, praying and crying. They held hands and just looked at the screen, so we just stayed like that for a long time. Then it seemed like it was alright to turn off the machine and we got our hearts ready to accept the inevitable. I got them settled in, and we decided to try and get a little sleep while we could.

Early the next morning, labor was more intense. She got into the tub for a couple of hours, and when the time was right, she gently pushed out their baby. His tiny body was perfect in every way, and he was completely still. The afterbirth came easily, it had been separated for a day already. We were all quiet while I tied the cord and dad cut it. We wrapped him in a white gauze cloth and dad held him while I got mama out of the tub. She got cleaned up and dressed, then used the bathroom and got into bed. I left them alone to go make us all breakfast. When I came back in the room to bring them their food, they were still holding him and just looking at their tiny boy. While they ate I weighed him and did his footprints. He was one pound even, then he was re-wrapped in a clean cloth. Mom and dad called him by name, and as they got ready to go home they never put him down. Mom would pass him to dad to do something and then get him back when she was done.

When their driver arrived, they gathered their belongings. We put their tiny baby boy in a small box and they left. I stood on the porch and watched them walk down the sidewalk to the car. To look at them now, no one would ever know that they were going home to bury their baby. I waved good bye to them and went back into the house. I walked back into the guest room to clean, and just stood for a few minutes and remembered the last eighteen hours. Then I tucked that memory in my heart and got busy doing my chores. Losing a child had to be one of the hardest things a parent could ever have to do. It was also a hard thing for the midwife to experience. There were so many unanswered questions... we had no control over death, but we did have the blessed assurance that one day we would all be together again, in the sweet by and by.

"For I am certain that nothing can separate us from His love: neither death nor life, neither angels nor other heavenly rulers or powers, neither the present nor the future, neither the world above nor the world below — there is nothing in all creation that will ever be able to separate us from the love of God which is ours through Christ Jesus our Lord." Romans 8:37-39 Good News Translation

LOUANNA

Gracious warrior, brave woman

Their baby was due the day after Christmas. That day came and went but it wasn't unusual for a first baby. She and her husband were confident and trusted that baby would come when the time was right. So, on New Year's Eve, that baby decided it was time. We stayed in touch through the day; things seemed to be progressing normally and she was staying busy. I wondered if this baby would be born this year, or next year. Since labor had started early in the morning, I was guessing probably next year. The few New Year's Eve babies I had attended, had all been born early in the day, not after dark. I had New Year's Day babies too, but they were born in the evening so I always got to ring in the New Year with my Hubby! This birth could be my first near midnight baby! I got excited about the possibility of a tax deduction for the family, or the honor of having the first baby of the year, but either way it would be a blessing. I gave my assistant the heads up and she was excited too since she had taught their childbirth classes.

Around supper time she was ready for me to come over and told me that her husband was on his way home from work. Once again, I left my Hubby to make his own dinner and I headed out the door. I called my assistant while I was driving to their house and told her to head that way too. As I drove I thought that I would probably miss bringing in this year with my Hubby. When I arrived at her house, she sounded serious but was completely focused and relaxing through contractions. She moved, walked, rested and snacked... she was doing all the right things. So much excitement to finally see who this child was!

The bedroom was all ready for the birth of the baby. My assistant and I were helping to encourage her, along with her husband. We all gave her sips of water and helped her change positions. We took turns rubbing her back and offered her snacks to keep her energy up, all the usual labor duties. Maybe we would see this baby before midnight! Even though she was working hard, she trusted her body and surrendered to what it was doing. Contractions got much more intense after the water broke, and less than two hours later she started pushing. She was so strong and worked perfectly with her body. We could see progress with every push and the baby sounded good during the first hour, then the baby's heart rate started to drop. Mama changed positions and my assistant put the oxygen on her. We could see the baby's head and its scalp color was good, but we continued to listen to the baby and thought it would be born within a few minutes. We were all four praying and with the next push the heart rate went down a little more. Sometimes this happens because the baby's head is getting squeezed.

When that contraction was finished the baby started sounding better, but the rate was still too low for my comfort, so I told them we needed to get the baby out and asked them if I could cut an episiotomy. They could hear the baby's heart rate as well as I could and knew there was a problem. They agreed, "Get the baby out!" So, my assistant handed me the scissors... my thoughts were accusing me, "mamas don't need to be cut..." I could count on one hand the number of times I had done it, but this baby needed to come out quickly. So, I took a deep breath and did what I had to and within the next minute, she had their precious baby in her arms, pink and screaming! "Thank you, Jesus!" rang out in the room, then tears of joy filled everyone's eyes. All the grandparents in the next room were singing their hallelujahs too. They had a tax deduction, just eighteen minutes before midnight. That was my last baby of the year. I think I texted my Hubby, "Happy New Year", a few minutes after midnight and he was excited to hear that the baby was born last year.

We got mom stitched up and fed. Baby was checked over too and everybody was doing great. All the grandparents were in love with their first grandbaby. After the cleaning and laundry and getting mom up to the bathroom, the new family was tucked into bed and baby was nursing. My assistant and I packed up our bags, loaded the cars and headed back home to our families in the early morning hours before daylight. It seemed that I was out driving at that time of night a lot. Through town the traffic lights were flashing, businesses were closed and there were very few cars on the roads. When I turned into my driveway and my car lights shone across the hay field, I saw a couple of deer startle and run. The house was dark when I came in from my night at work. I could hear my Hubby gently snoring as I tiptoed into the bedroom. He woke up and asked how it went. "A little scary for a minute, but mama and baby are doing great!" "That's good." He said and was back asleep. I, on the other hand, would need to unwind before I could sleep. So, I showered and got ready for bed and made myself a snack. Maybe I would just sit and watch the sunrise and praise my Lord for His mercies that are new every morning.

"Dear brothers and sisters, when troubles of any kind come your way, consider it an opportunity for great joy. For you know that when your faith is tested, your endurance has a chance to grow." James 1:2 New Living Translation

.

Made in the USA
Columbia, SC
18 February 2020